Chicken Logic

****

DISCARDED

Poems by

Gail Rixen

Winner of the 1996 SIDEWALKS Chapbook Contest

A *SIDEWALKS* publication
Copyright © 1996

Front Cover art by Ross Zirkle
Edited by Tom Heie
Artist photograph by Tim Kroeger
Other photographs by Darlene Joecks

"Delusions of the Master" first appeared in *North Coast Review*.

ISBN: 0-9656210-0-6

SIDEWALKS
                P. O. Box 321, Champlin, MN 55316

Copyright © 1997

Chicken Logic

Poems by Gail Rixen

Dedicated to the memory of Mari Thorndycraft

"Man, creature of God, who taught you friendship? A dog."

Arsène Houssaye

Contents

Early Lambing 1
On the Stand 2
After Junebugs 3
Chicken Logic 4
Tracking 5
Wolf is a Singular Noun 7
Alberta Clipper 8
Tinsel 9
The Fish Hatchery 10
Caged Cougar 12
Delusions of the Master 13
Contentment 14
In the Darwinian Court 15
Two Weeks of Deep Cold 16
Dammed River 17
The Kill 18
Stray 19
Work Horses 20
Essence 21
Spiders 22
Fifty-Three Below 23

EARLY LAMBING

March comes in spiteful.
As cold bites into my closed-off rooms,
walls crack loudly.
I gasp awake
and trudge outside to poke lambs
just to see them move.

Ten below.
They dig deep into straw.
The uninvited few outside
lean against shed siding,
their hooves torturing snow.
The sound echoes inside
like the croak of the dying.

Staring at shaking lambs,
I curse the buck, the weather, my thin walls.
Little ones, this is all my fault!

When light comes,
they stretch and shake off,
gaze wondering at this creature
who babbles as she rides the gate,
necessary as *The New York Times*
to a sheep's morning.

ON THE STAND

Chickadees are working
faster than my thoughts,
which plod through a thick woods
deep in snow,
coming back on their own dragging tracks
to plot them again.

Chickadees whir, circle limbs,
peck at bark upside down.
What little dry fare sustains those wings
wouldn't be enough for me.
I survive on greater things
that move through the dark unseen,
that know me for what I am,
not for all my wanting and doing,
not for all the self that stands here,
undone in a skin that collects her.

A chickadee perches on my head a moment
and moves on.
So slow are the movements of those
who want too much;
so light are the wings of those
who can make do.

AFTER JUNEBUGS

Long after junebugs
thud their desperate fingernails
against window screens,
after the dog has dug
its night hole in cool dirt,
after the moon has drawn
the soft edges of window frames
into a dark room,
the tired human tongue rests.

In the quiet we learn again
to touch the fuzzy edges of sense,
refine the creature's busy muscles
to the simplest grace.

The day lies down with memory
to conceive an honest answer
to the far owl's question,
Who are you?

CHICKEN LOGIC

Hunched like disgruntled men
along main street,
chickens line up under the granary overhang
as October snow falls in blowzy flakes.
Maybe in chicken logic,
anything can be endured
on one leg.

An economy of gizzard-gravel
and tomato seeds.
In rain, hunt earthworms.
In drought, grasshoppers.
Toes and comb are expendable
in a cold winter.

Today the televised debate
is over who looks good
in the latest polls.
Oh, let us cock our heads
and change legs.

TRACKING

We take turns from blood drop
to reddened twig,
stepping beside the tracks
that head, straight as resolve,
to deeper woods.

The doe is hit.
Fawns follow, try other paths,
and return to her slowing steps.

Fingers that pulled the trigger
hold brush against their light skin
to find the red.
"Meat, too," he says.

We lose the blood trail
and stand still in the snow.
So many tracks now and no blood.
We bumble about,
obliterating the fine molds
with our huge bootsteps.

Circling wider and wider,
he finds her bloody beds.
At last, we sigh;
she can't go far now.

But she does.
Her last blood doesn't show again,
on any trail,
though we double back
and follow any tracks again,
in deep, far from men and industry,
past river meanders and frozen swamps.
Into tangled brush.
Through cattails.

When we return, disgruntled,
to her beds,
we say nothing.
He looks up into the grey overhang of limbs,
half expecting her,
whole and magical,
high up.

WOLF IS A SINGULAR NOUN

After the coyotes
have ended their adolescent pep fest
and gone on down their moon-blued paths,
the basso wolf sits on its lonely trail
and howls its complaint.

Walking to the neighbors' lit house,
my partner and I howl back in duet,
a burlesque of the solitary.

We don't wait for reply.

ALBERTA CLIPPER

All night gusts slam full-bodied against the house.
Wind huffs down the chimney,
Freddie Krueger at the flue cover,
and insists against pliant window glass.
In the cookstove, wood burns up paper-fast,
leaving no remnant in the room but draft.
Clouds bolt, one by panicked one,
past a blank moon.
Power lines swing madly between poles
and lights flicker so often,
I finally go to bed.
Even the dog sleeps fitfully.

In the morning the answer machine,
remembering the last human voice,
counts four messages.
They all say, "Run."

TINSEL

The years planes flew over
going northwest
they dropped something like tinsel,
which was practice, we figured,
to fool the Commies,
having been taught to foil them
by diving under our desks.
Straight white jet trails,
sonic booms in clear afternoons,
safe another day.

Nothing came of it,
even after we got television.
Harvest followed summer,
planting followed snow,
birdsnests woven with silver strands.

THE FISH HATCHERY

On cold spring nights
a man sits with the fish eggs
below the Fish Hook dam
beside the park.
It's water temperature, sound, and sunlight,
he explains to those who come touring,
who haven't sat up nights
with the moon and the running water
and the late chill creaking the roof timbers
and the stillness of a town asleep
all around him up the hill.

He will be ninety soon.
Grey and thin and green and strong,
he defeats the young death he was born to,
wandering between the tanks
of some things becoming something else entirely.
Shuffling to keep warm,
he waits as he has for deer and bear,
thinking, wiping thinking free, and dreaming.

Children come even now
to park their cars
in the Saturday night hollow,
not knowing he sits there.
They wriggle in their human skins,
twist and twine on the upholstery.
The windows fog.
The water runs.
He nods and wakes.

Broken ice bobs and scrapes against the dam.
High water strains against cement.
The eggs hear, and stir,
too big for their shells.
He can't nap tonight,
when all around him is uncurling
and stirring and straining,
too big, too full again
of water and air and life.

CAGED COUGAR

Pop the eardrums of the sentry.
Tunnel the sight of a hunter.
Throw dust into nostrils,
on the tongue.
Make the little world smooth,
easy to clean.
Stifle the opportune wind.
Stop doing.
End trying.

Leave only the being.
Relentless being.
Strange voices sieved through iron bars
to gibberish.

Only the being left.
The being.

DELUSIONS OF THE MASTER

In a just rage,
I scatter mothballs in the dog-dug holes
under the picnic table,
in the flower beds.
I shake my fist,
threaten dire consequences.
They cozy up or hide,
reading the crazy woman's tones,
my words, gibberish.
My logical explanations
just widen the innocent eyes.

All day they jump from their mud beds
and lie back down when I pass.
They earnestly follow me
about my worthy work,
snuff dutifully down every hole I dig.
At the end of the day,
they slide their contrite heads
under my hand.
I lean over them,
the Alpha,
the asshole.

CONTENTMENT

Two sheep racing past the gate,
kicking up their heels,
shouted back to me,
"One pair for the ground;
one for the air."

A brown hawk holding fast
to the high cottonwood
in yellow morning sun
aimed her vivid eye and declared,
"I have flown my vigil in the fields
and found you."

One wren, like one last leaf,
flipping from walnut twig to bare bough,
couldn't settle long,
but whistled,
"So much luxury in the day."

The old tomcat,
his ears frozen down to stubs,
his face askew with scars,
slid along my leg,
saying in his throaty brogue,
"You're beautiful, you know.
Just lovely."

As I watched from the barn loft,
the blue-lidded moon
patiently placed little lights
across the face of the prairie
and all of them whispered together
across the still night,
"We are here
and you are among us."

IN THE DARWINIAN COURT

Despised and forsaken of chickens,
the young rooster froze to death
in the grain trough
with a full crop,
losing to the terrible social ratio
of three roosters to five hens.

The hens, however,
grew fat in the herded harem.
On the question of fairness
they had no opinion.

TWO WEEKS OF DEEP COLD

No tracks in snow.
Birds tore even the rose hips open
and went away hungry.
Every living thing
is hunkered down,
trying to dream.

I find a mouse frozen
in its corn-pail heaven.

As I flounder
through thigh-high snow,
a raven flies over
squawking,
Throw Out Your Dead.

Keep Moving
pounds like an alarm
through my veins.

DAMMED RIVER

Water gathers in the old oxbows.
Memory in the banks,
the river contracts back into its spring
and slows.
No energy left in the coil,
water greens,
oozes from the beaver dam
thick, dropless.

A beaver crosses its pool,
parting the gloss into two bodied lines
that roll to the ruined shore,
bumping,
disappearing.

THE KILL

When the dogs team up
against woodchuck and muskrat,
one makes the grab
and one, the kill.
In a frenzy of howls, squeals,
whines and growls,
they bite and shake it,
stretch it between them
and tear and shake
till the joints come loose,
then with methodical jaws,
crunch it from head to tail,
toss and shake the bag
which gives no resistance,
and drop it in the sun to puff up.

Now they tremble from the old drug,
must sit and pant in the shade
to become your pet again,
the ones who take scraps
from your bare hand.

STRAY

There's a black dog in the neighborhood.
Nobody's dog,
living on garbage and roadkill.
Chased away,
scared of doors opening.
Comes by night to steal
and leave turd piles
on doorsteps, pet dishes, lawn ornaments.

Someone should do something.
Not me. I haven't been out
since I shut the door
seven years ago.
My neighbors never see
when the dog passes through
the light squares
their windows glare onto the ground.
I see. I leave my lights out.

I watch it going away down the ditch.
Snow coming down so thick today
it's barely anything after a while.

No reason to shovel the walk.

WORK HORSES

When there's talk of the big horses,
he doesn't say much,
ever since the fifties
when he stopped skidding out logs
and sold the old dapple.

Because he could show you scars.
They stepped on your feet,
kicked you, threw you,
spooked at nothing,
and ate up your profits.
And so blasted slow.

He names them,
always in pairs, like harmony,
Prince and Mick,
Dick and Daisy,
Florie and Fannie,
Lady and May,
forgetting himself in the old chants.
Lay the reins out slack
and they did the rest.
"When I slapped her flank,
she grunted against the singletree,
and bent it, pulling,
and brought the widow-makers down."
Shakes his head. The power.

Then always:
"Sure an improvement
when we got the tractor."

ESSENCE

My hay being too poor,
I feed corn
to get the milking ewes through
a winter of all-time record cold.
In a day, the shed goes sour.
The simple scent of timothy and clover,
taken over by some fermented industry.

Out in the open air,
I want to outrun my coveralls,
get clean away from love gone rank,
good intentions turned foul,
things going bad,
all of it last year's sileage
to chew on this winter.

Seeing me,
the neighbor's dog
raises her nose into the air
to test the truth
I can't help but tell:
What kind of thing have you been?

SPIDERS

Flies, slowed by the cool air of the house
or singed by the light bulb,
bumble about into the corners,
wandering until they are hopelessly tangled
and sucked dry by the light climbers
who bind their husks in dusty sarcophagi
and hang them upside down.

In January cold, assorted hefts of spiders
live closer to the cookstove.
Sometimes I blunder, morning-mean,
through tender nets tied across doorways.
Dammit! I sweep the warm rooms down,
but they are back again,
more asymmetrical every day,
strung in a reckless rage by moonlight.
Take that, broom woman!

By the time weather tames,
they have all the flies
and some of their own
strung like puppets
that bob in the wake of my passing.

FIFTY-THREE BELOW

Melting deep into their snow beds
in the cedar swamp,
deer wait out the coldest night.
Moonlight nudges under cedar boughs
and cold cracks its way into trees,
a sharp cry in the silence,
as though the whole woods
is breaking apart,
shadow by shadow.

Nothing is going anywhere
but the cars that growl and wheeze,
searching the night with tunnel vision.

By now the deer,
only a ravine away,
know my voice
nightly advertising my gift of grass hay
that every morning lies untouched.
By dawn,
their iced impressions are empty.
Trails head on.
The kindest thing I do
is keep to my side of the fence.

Gail Rixen has lived and worked in northern and west central Minnesota as a finish carpenter and teacher. She co-owns a farm near Nebish.

Gail's work has appeared in magazines and anthologies, and her book of poems, *Pictures of Three Seasons*, was published by New Rivers Press in 1991.

NORMANDALE COMMUNITY COLLEGE
LIBRARY
9700 FRANCE AVENUE SOUTH
BLOOMINGTON, MN 55431-4399